Level 2

The Nature Kid's Guide to
SNAILS AND SLUGS

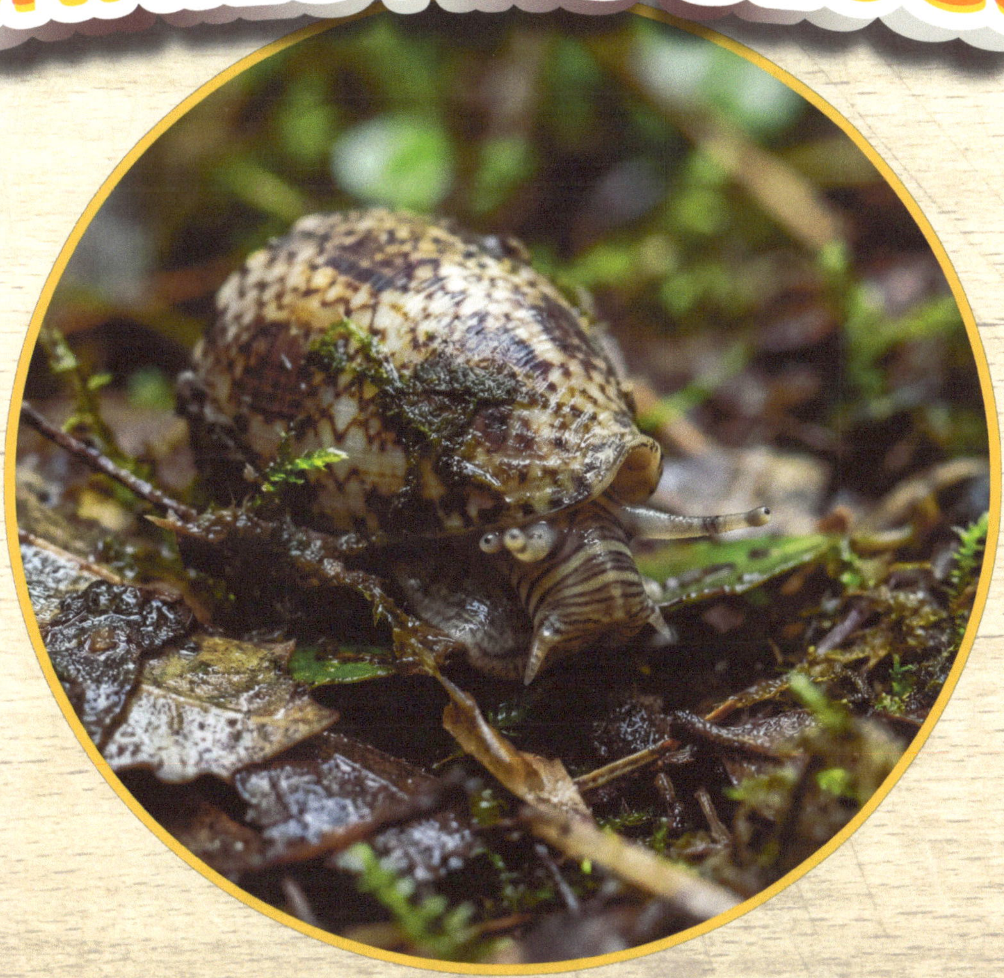

DAVID ANDERSON

LP Media Inc. Publishing
Text copyright © 2026 by LP Media Inc.
All rights reserved.

For information address LP Media Inc. Publishing,
30012 Variolite St NW, Princeton MN 55371
www.lpmedia.org

Publication Data

Snails and Slugs
The Nature Kid's Guide to Snails and Slugs — First edition.

Summary: "Learn all about Snails and Slugs, the Nature Kid Way"
— Provided by publisher.

ISBN: 979-8-89818-216-8

[1. Snails and Slugs – Non-Fiction] I. Title.

Title: The Nature Kid's Guide to Snails and Slugs

CONTENTS

STOMACH WALKERS

Squish! A snail slides across a wet garden leaf at dawn.

Pick up a rock in your garden after a rainstorm and you might find one — a slow, slimy, surprisingly fascinating creature that has been crawling across the Earth for over 500 million years.

Snails and slugs live on every continent except Antarctica. They thrive in gardens, forests, tide pools, and the deep ocean. Snails carry a shell on their back. Slugs do not. Both walk on a single flat muscle called a foot — right on their belly.

Scientists call them **gastropods**. It means stomach foot. It is the perfect name for these interesting (and slimy) creatures.

SPIRAL SECRETS
FUN FACT!
Most snail shells spiral to the right, but about 1 in 10,000 curl left!

Crack! A tiny snail pokes out from a shell no bigger than a pea.

A snail's shell is its home. The shell is hard and keeps the snail safe inside. It is made of calcium, just like your bones.

As the snail grows, so does its shell. New rings form at the edge over time. Most shells curl in a spiral shape, round and round.

When danger comes, a snail can pull its whole body inside. This helps it hide from birds and other hungry animals. The shell is like a tiny fortress that goes everywhere the snail goes!

SHELL OPTIONAL

Splat! A banana slug squeezes under a damp rock to hide from the sun.

Slugs look like snails without shells. Long ago, the first slugs did have shells. Over millions of years, some lost them completely.

Without a shell, a slug can fit into tight spaces. It slips under logs, rocks, and bark with ease. This helps it find food in places snails cannot reach.

But slugs must stay wet. They dry out fast in the sun. So most slugs come out at night or after rain, hiding in dark, damp spots all day long.

SLIME TIME
DID YOU KNOW?
A snail can slide upside down across a ceiling, held up only by its slime!
10

Shlurp! A slug oozes a thick trail of slime across the garden path.

Snails and slugs make slime with their whole body. This slime is called **mucus**. It helps them in many neat ways.

Slime keeps their soft skin wet. It also helps them slide along the ground without getting stuck. A snail can even glide over a sharp razor blade without getting cut!

Some slime tastes bad to animals that want to eat them. Other slime fights off germs. Slime is a real superpower for these small creatures.

SLIMY SURFERS

A garden snail moves about 50 yards per hour, which means a snail race could take all day!

Swish! Two long tentacles wave in the air, testing for smells.

Snails and slugs move in a neat way. Tiny muscles ripple under their big flat foot, pushing them along their slime trail bit by bit.

Land snails have four **tentacles** on their head. The top two hold tiny eyes at the tips. The bottom two help them smell and feel things around them.

Sea snails often have just two tentacles. But all snails and slugs rely on touch and smell to find food and stay safe. Their eyes can only see light and dark.

RASPING RIBBONS

Scritch! A snail scrapes its tiny teeth across a fresh green leaf.

Snails and slugs eat with a special tongue called a **radula**. It is like a ribbon covered with rows of tiny teeth.

The radula works like sandpaper. A snail rubs it back and forth across its food, scraping up leaves, fruit, and even tree bark. You can sometimes hear a snail eating if you listen closely!

Some snails eat other animals too. A few kinds hunt worms and small bugs. The radula helps them break up many kinds of meals.

DART ROMANCE

16

Plink! Two snails touch tentacles and begin a very strange dance.

Most snails and slugs are both male and female at the same time. This means any two snails can be parents together!

When garden snails meet, one may shoot a tiny dart at the other. The dart is like a small, pointy stick made of calcium. It does not hurt, but it helps the eggs stay healthy.

After mating, the snail digs a small hole and lays round, soft eggs in the dirt. In a few weeks, tiny babies hatch and crawl away.

GARDEN GLIDERS
FUN FACT!
Garden snails first came from Europe and now live on six continents, everywhere except Antarctica!

Crunch! A garden snail munches on a ripe berry in the cool grass.

Garden snails are one of the most common snails in the world. You may have seen one in your own yard! Their shells are brown with dark swirly stripes.

These snails eat plants, fruit, and dead leaves. They come out in the evening and after rain. In hot, dry weather, they seal their shell with dry slime and take a long nap that can last for months.

Garden snails can live up to five years. Birds, frogs, and beetles all love to eat them, but their hard shells help keep them safe.

LAND GIANTS

DID YOU KNOW?

One Giant African land snail can lay over 1,200 eggs in a single year, enough to fill a shoebox!

Thud! A snail as big as a softball crawls across a thin branch.

Giant African land snails are one of the biggest land snails on Earth. Their shells can grow up to eight inches long. That is about the size of your whole hand!

These huge snails live in warm parts of Africa. They eat over 500 kinds of plants, munching on soft tree bark and flowers too.

People have taken them to other countries as pets. But there, they eat too much and grow out of control. Many places now work hard to stop them from spreading.

DEADLY BEAUTIFUL

Cone snail venom contains over 100 different chemicals, and scientists use it to make new medicines!

Zap! A cone snail slides along the ocean floor. Fish swim away fast!

Cone snails live in warm oceans near coral reefs. They have pretty shells with bright patterns. But do not touch one! These snails are fierce hunters.

A cone snail has a sharp tooth shaped like a tiny tube. It shoots this tooth out like a dart, and the tooth is filled with **venom** that stuns a fish in seconds.

Some cone snails can even hurt people. Their sting causes great pain and can be deadly. Divers learn to look at them but never, ever pick them up.

BANANA BONANZA
DID YOU KNOW?
The banana slug is the official mascot of the University of California, Santa Cruz!

Plop! A big yellow slug drops from a fern onto the forest floor.

Banana slugs are bright yellow, just like a ripe banana. Some have dark brown spots too. They are one of the biggest slugs in the world, growing up to ten inches long.

These slugs live in cool, wet forests in western North America. They love rain and shade. Dead leaves and mushrooms are their favorite foods.

Banana slugs help the forest in a big way. They eat dead plants and turn them into rich soil. Trees and flowers grow better thanks to these slimy helpers.

TIGER STRIPES

Rustle! A striped snail as big as a fist creeps out at night.

Giant tiger land snails have bold stripes on their shells. The stripes are dark brown and gold, like a tiger's fur. These snails live in the forests of West Africa.

At night, they crawl out to find food. They eat fruit, leaves, and even bits of bone for calcium. The calcium makes their big shells strong and thick.

Sadly, these snails are getting hard to find. People hunt them for food, and forests are being cut down. Keeping their homes safe is very important for their future.

SEA SLUGS

FUN FACT!
There are over 3,000 kinds of nudibranchs, and scientists discover new ones every year!

Bubble! A bright pink sea slug glides through the warm, clear reef.

Nudibranchs are sea slugs with no shell at all. Their name means bare gills. They come in wild colors like blue, pink, purple, and bright orange.

These bold colors warn other animals to stay away. Many nudibranchs have poison in their skin that tastes very bad. Fish learn quickly not to eat them.

Nudibranchs live in oceans all over the world. Some are as small as a grain of rice. Others can grow as long as your arm! Each one looks like a tiny underwater jewel.

DRAGON DRIFTERS

Blue dragons sometimes wash up on beaches by the hundreds after big storms!

Whoosh! A tiny blue slug floats upside down on the ocean waves.

Blue dragon sea slugs are tiny but fierce. They are only about one inch long. Their bright blue and silver body looks like a little dragon with feathery wings.

These slugs float upside down on the sea. An air bubble in their belly keeps them at the top, and wind and waves push them from place to place.

Blue dragons eat stinging jellyfish, including the deadly Portuguese man-of-war. They save the stings inside their own body. Then they can sting anything that tries to eat them!

FIRE SNAILS

32

Flash! A jet black shell glides through the mist on a bright red foot.

Deep in the cool cloud forests of Malaysia, high above the jungle floor, lives one of the most striking snails on Earth. The Malaysian fire snail has a bold jet black shell and a foot so bright red it looks like it is on fire.

This snail lives in just one small area of the world — a stretch of misty mountain forest about 100 miles wide. It needs cool temperatures and high humidity to survive. Take it out of those conditions and it quickly dies.

Because of its beauty, people smuggle fire snails to sell as pets. This is pushing the species toward extinction.

ROMAN RANCHERS

People in France eat about 30,000 tons of cooked snails, called escargot, every year!

Scrape! A plump snail chews a wild herb on a sunny hillside.

Roman snails have big, round shells with cream and brown bands. They live in grassy fields and open forests across Europe.

Long ago, the Romans raised these snails for food. They kept them in special snail gardens called cochlearia. That is how these snails got their name, over 2,000 years ago!

Today, Roman snails are protected in many countries. It is against the law to pick them up in some places. People want to make sure they stay safe in the wild for years to come.

NATURE'S HELPERS

Munch! A snail glides under a log, eating every leaf in its path.

Snails and slugs play a big role in nature. They are food for many animals. Birds, frogs, turtles, and beetles all count on them for meals.

These slow crawlers also help plants spread to new places. Seeds stick to their slime as they travel. They carry the seeds far away without even knowing it!

Snail and slug droppings add good things to the soil, helping plants grow strong. Without these slimy helpers, nature would not work as well.

SLIMY SURVIVORS

Patter! Rain falls and snails wake up, ready for a fresh night out.

Snails and slugs are some of the toughest survivors on Earth — they outlasted the dinosaurs and kept going through every disaster this planet has thrown at them.

But today, some kinds are in trouble. Pollution poisons the wet places they need to live. Forests get cut down.

You can help by leaving damp, wild corners of your yard alone and skipping the bug spray.

So next time you find one in your garden, take a moment to look closely. There is a lot more going on under that shell than most people ever stop to notice!

GLOSSARY

gastropod

An animal with a soft body and a flat foot, like snails and slugs

mucus

Thick, slippery slime that an animal's body makes

radula

A tongue-like ribbon covered with tiny teeth, used to scrape food

tentacle

A long, thin body part used to touch and smell things

venom

A poison some animals use to stun or hurt other animals